AF322651

I Like Being Different

Author: Blu Semper

Co Author: Athyn Semper

Dad says theres something special about me. Not the kind that means something might be wrong, no no no something reeeeal special. I was wanted so much that special things were done to get me here!

See I learned that even though every kid got here in a different way, every kid comes with LOVE! After all isn't love what really matters? My friends and I all look different. Some us have curly hair, some of us straight. Some of us have freckles, some of us dimples. Some of us have dark skin, some of us light. We are all different, be we all come from LOVE.

I asked my parents what it meant to come from love and they both had different answers. Mommy said it meant that two people decided to bring a baby into the world to make it a better place. Daddy said it meant that the universe knew it was time for a family to grow. I don't really know what all of that stuff means, but I know how good I feel when they tell me they love me. So I believe its when a family has extra hugs and kisses to give away.

Sometimes kids look like one parent, sometimes they look like both. Isn't it strange when kids don't look like either parent? I used to think so, but not anymore. Not since I found out how cool it was to be different.

Everyone always tells me how lucky I am that soooo many people love me. Isn't this normal guys? I guess not *shrugs*. I mean I'd say I'm pretty special, I've got two moms, a dad, three grandmas, and three god parents! Whoaw! I haven't even counted my aunts, uncles and all my cousins. That's a looooot of LOVE! I guess I really am lucky, maybe even DIFFERENT!

Does all this family and love really make me different? Am I different because there's so much love for me? At first, I thought that maybe there was too much LOVE. Maybe I should give some back. Then, I probably wouldn't be different. That wasn't it! I was different for a whole other reason. I like dancing, gymnastics and cooking, not every kid likes that. Maybe this makes me different. Nope, not that either. I do meditation to go to bed and recite my mantras every morning. Every kid doesn't do that, surely this makes me so different! Nope, not that either!

I'm out of ideas! What makes me so different? Dad says when I get a little bigger he'll explain. But I'm big now! I wanna know now!

Will this difference make a difference? Will it change things? Will I still get a lot of LOVE? Will I still have all my family and best friends?

I've decided tomorrow is the day! Tomorrow, I'm going to be big enough to know! I'm gonna go to bed, and when I wake up I'll be big enough! Yup! Tomorrow is D Day!

Riiiiing, goes the alarm. *Yawns* It's D Day! *Jumps out of bed with excitement*Daddy! Daddy! Daddy! Guess what! What is it baby? What is it!? He asked. It's D Day! I said. What's D Day you ask? D Day is TODAY, the day that I'm big enough to find out what makes me different.

Daddy takes a long look at me, stares at me straight in my eyes and smiles. He tucks his hands underneath my underarms , picks me up and spins me around. (loud laughing). "Daddy, stop it you're gonna make us dizzy!" I yell. I couldn't control the laughter. I love when he does it. I feel like a bird! I feel free! Got it! THIS, is why I'm different. None of my other friends feel like animals I don't think.

Finally, he puts me down. He kissed me on my forehead, lifted my chin and said "baby girl, today isn't the day. I'm sorry but you're still not big enough." "Hmmmph!" was my only response. With folded arms and a frowned face I sighed and went back to my room.

While sitting on my bed it came to me. Hey, today is Saturday. On Saturdays my friend Malia comes over. Malia is my very best friend. She has two moms and they both work on Saturday, so she spends the day with us until one or both of them get off. My dad is really good friends with Ashley that's Malia's mommy. He knew her first. Then he met Shane, that Malia's other mom. They're really fun! When they get off of work they come over and sometimes bring pizza, we sing karaoke or play monopoly. If me and Malia did good in school that week, we get to have a sleep over for the night. One night at my house, one night at hers.

Malia's moms only let her sleep at my house. They say they love her too much to let her sleep just anywhere. She has to be with someone they fully trust. Hmmmm, that's kinda like how all my parents love me. Hey, I wonder if Malia thinks she's different too. I've got it! Malia must know. I'm gonna ask her when she gets here.

"Andiiiii, Andi baby, Andi come here" I heard daddy calling from the living room. "Yes daddy" I said. "Hey baby, so I have great news and not so good news. What do you want first?" he asked. "Ummm great?" I said. " Ok, today we're going to Archer's place. "Ummmm great?" I shrugged. "Ok today we're going to Archer's Place!" he said. "Yes! (Dancing and jumping with excitement) woohoo, I can't wait for Malia to get here! Wait, I gotta call her and tell her to wear the same bathing suit as me!" I yelled. "Wait, wait, baby wait just a second." He said. "Huh?" I responded. "Malia isn't coming today," said daddy. "Why? Is she sick? Maybe she doesn't know the good news." I said. "No no baby, Malia's moms took her to see her grandma in New Jersey. They'll be there for the weekend" he said. "Oh, ok" (sadly) I responded. "Hey, what's the matter, you don't wanna hang out with just your dad today? We haven't done that in a long time" he said. "No, no, no daddy, I like" I said. Daddy laughed hard. He looks at me and says "you like me? You like me! Girl you better looooooooove me!" (He grabs me and starts tickling me while I laugh uncontrollably). "Ok! Ok! Ok! I love you! I love! I really, really, love you! He continues to tickle me down to the floor. "You betta!" he yells at me. He squeezed me tight and gave me a big kiss on my forehead and said "ok go grab some stuff to wear and let me see so we can pack a bag to go." "Ok daddy!" I said and hopped up off the floor and ran in the room.

I love Archer's Place! But Malia won't be there, so I won't get to ask her about being different. Well, I guess I'll just ask her at school on Monday (shrugs). "I'm going to Archer's Place!" I whispered. I pull out an outfit to wear, my favorite Shisho bathing suit with the hat and slippers to match and another outfit incase this one gets messed up. Daddy always says, "make sure you have back up Andi." I grabbed my favorite Shisho towel with the goggles to match and ran into daddy's room. "Daddy, I got everything!" I screamed. "Ok baby, lets see what you got" he replies. He goes through my stuff and looks at me and smiles. "You're becoming such a big girl Andi. It's like you're not even my baby girl anymore." I grab his hand and pull him down to me and do what he always does to me. I raise his face by his chin and say "daddy, you know I'll always be your #1 baby girl, right?" "Yes" he replies. "Good! Now who's my #1 big guy?" I ask. (While laughing loudly because he sees where I'm going with this) "me" he says. I look him square in the eye and ask "am I too big to hang out with my favorite guy today? You're gonna get a new baby? Maybe I should call my uncle!" "No, no, no, I like you. I like hanging out with you" he replies. I stare him straight in the eye and say "you like hanging out with me? You better loooove hanging out with me" immediately followed by tickling. He started laughing so loud he couldn't control it. "ok, ok I love hanging out with you! You're my #1 baby girl" he yells. "You betta!" I shout. I grabbed his face and gave him a kiss on the forehead and said "time to go." He starts helping me get dressed, and once I'm done, he takes me in the living room to go finish getting his bag together.

After he was done, he came out with two small bags. One with his change of clothes, and one with all the "important" stuff. He puts the bag with all the important stuff in front of me and says "ok baby lets do a checklist to make sure we have what we NEED while we're there. "ok" I said. "Ok, when I call out the item you look in the bag and if it's in there you say CHECK! If its not there, you say MISSING, bet?" "Bet!" I replied.

One by one he started calling out the items. "Sunscreen?" "CHECK!", "Band-Aids?" "CHECK!", "Alcohol pads?" "CHECK!", "Lotion?" "CHECK!", "Goggles?" "CHECK!", "Andi's favorite swim cap?" "MISSING!" I forgot my Shisho swim cap! I ran into the room to grab it and couldn't find it. I ran back to tell daddy that I couldn't find it and he replied "its ok baby we'll get a new one when we get there. "ok" I said. "Now lets finish the list so we can get on the road."

He said. "Booger-sucker?" "Eww daddy! CHECK!" I picked it up with two fingers and waived it at him. "You won't say that when you get out the water and you can't breathe" he chuckled. "Ha, ha, ha" I said. "Ok, we've got everything we need. Let's put our shoes on and hit the road" he said.

I shook my head yes and we both got up. He grabbed his bag and important bag, his phone and his keys. I got my backpack and put it on, and both walked toward the door. We put on our shoes, took one last look around to make sure nothing is left behind and walk out. As we walk down the hallway to the elevator, I race to push the button. I love pressing the buttons because I know exactly where we're going. After I pushed the button to go down, daddy grabbed a handful of mints that was in a bowl in front of the mirror right next to the elevators. He lives in a nice building, every floor has a bowl filled with mints on a stand in between the elevator doors. The lights are bright and inside the elevator when you press the button for a floor a lady comes on and says when you get to that floor, and also shows on a screen at the top. When you get all the way

downstairs, you can turn right and go to the gym or the pool; or turn left to go to the store or through the door to the garage. If you go straight out, you see Jaxon and Terry. They work at the front desk, and make sure that everybody that comes to the building has "god business" there. That's what Jaxon told me. Once we get off the elevator, we waived hi to both Jaxon and Terry and made the left for the garage. There's a secret code to the door that only the adults that have cars in there know ho to unlock. (It's so that no one can go in and steal somebody else's car)

We get to our car, daddy opens the trunk and puts all the bags in. He opens the door for me, and I hop in. "Buckle up cheeky" he says. He's been calling me that since I was a baby because he likes to squeeze my chubby cheeks. "All in" I replied. He opened the secret door in front of the seat next to him and pulled out my tablet and headphones and gave them to me. Then, he buckled his seatbelt, connected his phone to the car, put the address in the gps, turned on the music and pressed the button to open the garage door so we could drive out. I scrolled on my tablet to my favorite game, and just before I put my headphones on I heard the gps lady say "you should reach your destination by 10am." I smiled because that means we have all day to be at Archer's Place. I put my headphones on, and we were headed on our way. Just before we got to the exit of the garage, daddy stopped the car. I looked up and he was looking at me in the driving mirror. I saw him waving at me and his lips were moving. I took the headphones off and heard him saying "baby can you hear me?" "No daddy, I'm sorry I was playing my game" I replied. "It's ok, I forgot to ask before we left the house if you needed to use the bathroom?" he asked. "No daddy, I'm fine I used it when I went to get to my stuff." I said. "Are you sure cheeky? Cause I can pull over and we can go in the lobby bathroom real quick" he said. "No daddy, I'm ok." I replied. "Ok, because the gps says its gonna take about 1 whole hour to get there and you know I don't like those dirty bathrooms on the road for you" he said. "I know daddy, but I'm fine" I said. "Ok then, you can get back to your game" he says. I picked up my headphones, the music came back on, and I kept playing my game.

Long car rides sometimes make me sleepy, but not today! I'm too excited. I'm staying up the whole ride. I looked at the clock on the front of daddy's car and the time said 9:06. We have 54 minutes to get there. I played game after game suddenly we hit a bump. I turned my head and my headphones were on the seat next to me. I looked down at my hands and my tablet was on the floor. I looked up at daddy's driving mirror and he was smiling at me. "Hi sleepyhead! You're finally awake?" he asked. I was puzzled. I just knew I wasn't going to fall asleep; I was so excited. "Yes, I thought I was gonna stay up this time" I said. He chuckled and said "baby you know daddy's car has sleepy juice" we both laughed. I grabbed the cord of the headphones and pulled the tablet up from the floor and put it on the seat next to me. When I looked at the clock on the front of daddy's car it was 9:52. We are 8 minutes away!

I started seeing the big posters for Archer's Place and Shisho and Railey's face everywhere. I was smiling so much my cheeks started to hurt. I grabbed my sunglasses out of the pouch thingy behind the seat in front of me and put them on. Then I heard the gps lady say, "you've arrived at your destination."

I unfastened my seatbelt and grabbed my tablet and headphones dropped it in the front seat and grabbed the door handle. I looked really quickly to my left and daddy was staring at me through the driving mirror. He didn't have to say a word. I sat back down. I knew better. I'm supposed to wait until a grown up opens the door and let's me out. "Children aren't supposed to just get out of cars like that cheeky, sometimes bad things happen and you don't wanna get hurt" I can hear him clear as day and he hadn't said a word. He picked up my tablet from the seat and put it back in. "Thank You" he said. "I'm sorry daddy" I responded. "I know baby, I know you're excited. Just let daddy get out first and make sure its safe and then I'll get you out, ok?" "Ok daddy" I replied. He unplugged his phone, unhooked his seatbelt and got out the car. He walked around to the back, and then opened my door. "Excuse me young lady, I understand there is a princess Andi that's supposed to be here. Have you seen her?" I smiled wide and said "yes, it's me! I'm right here." He stretched his hand to me; I grabbed it and he led me out.

Daddy always says "when you get out of a car you look both ways, because another car may be near and not see you." I did just that! Daddy smiled "that's my cheeky!" He locked the car, switched hands so I was on his inside and we walked to the park entrance. The closer we got, the more excited I got, the faster I walked. Daddy looked down at me and said, "hey last one to the Archer sign is a rotten egg!" We both took off running. I beat him! I got there first! Daddy was the rotten egg. We laughed and hugged and posed for 3 silly face selfies.

After the pictures we headed into the park. Daddy walked up to a lady, showed her his phone and she pulled out 2 blue bracelets. One for me and one for him. " First stop is the store to get you a swim cap then we'll go change our clothes. Bet?" daddy said. "Bet" I said, and we bumped fists. We got into the store and I went straight to the swim

stuff. I didn't even check out the toys. I found the perfect swim cap and

met daddy at the counter. He paid for it and the lady asked if he needed

a bag. He looked down at me and asked, "what do you think cheeky,

we need a bag?" "No thank you!" I said. The lady at the counter laughed

and handed me the cap. "Thanks a lot lady!" I yelled while waiving and

dragging daddy out of the store.

Things always get tricky when its just me and daddy any time

we have to go to the bathroom, so we try to do the best we can at going

as least as possible. I already put my bathing suit on at home and he

already wore his swim shorts, so I just have to take my regular clothes

off. We both got fully prepared for water rides, switched out sneakers

for slippers, got our sunscreen and towels out, I put my swim cap on

and everything else went into the locker we stood in front of.

While daddy fixed the hook to his phone pouch I waited by the

locker. Just then I heard someone call out my name "Andi, Andi, hi

Andi!" It was my friend Gabriel! Oh boy this day just keeps getting

better and better. Gabriel said hi to my dad and my dad said "hey buddy,

good to see! Are you here with your parents?" "Yup! They're right

there. They're coming over now. I got excited when I saw Andi and came over to say hi" he said. Gabriel's parents walked over and were full of smiles. They are so cool, but so different from Gabriel. Gabriel's skin is dark like mine, but his parents are both white. They both work at our school, and they're the best chaperons for our class trips. One time on a trip Gabriel was crying at the back of the bus because some kids were bothering him about his parents not being the same color as him. I heard his mom tell his dad that "it breaks her heart because she loves him so much, she won't allow anyone to hurt him not even a child!" Hmmm my parents tell me that too! I've got it! Gabriel is gonna help me figure out what makes me different.

Gabriel's parents were two footsteps away and smiling really hard. It seems as though they were just as excited to see us as we were to see them. Gabriel's mom gave my dad and I a hug and his dad gave my dad a handshake, then me a hug. Our parents knew each other well from all the parent association stuff my dad goes to at the school. They spoke and laughed for a while and then they looked down at us. I guess they could tell we were ready to go. "Guess what Andi?" daddy asked. "What daddy?" I excitingly replied. "I guess you won't be alone on this trip after all. Gabriel and his parents just got here too, and they're going to all the areas we normally go to" daddy said. Me and Gabriel looked at each other, then hugged tightly while jumping up and down. "Yessss" we both yelled out. Gabriel's dad laughed out so hard he heled his stomach. He turned to my dad and said, "hey man we may get some really good Father's Day gifts this year!" Gabriel's mom and daddy started laughing too. Gabriel and I didn't really get the joke.

I grabbed Gabriel's hand, looked up at my dad and he said "not too far ahead of us guys, we need to be able to see you." "Ok dad!" I yelled. We took off running and ran straight across to wait at the gate to wait for them. When they got to us, we all walked in the gate and then placed the slippers and towels on the side.

This is my favorite part to start at. There's a huge slide, a net you can climb and a big bucket all in the water. Me and Gabriel went up and down the slide and climbed the net over and over again. It was so much fun. Our dads took pictures of us, while Gabriel's mom got in and played tag with us. When she got tired, she took the camera from his dad, and they switched places. We played the dunk contest, First Gabriel, then me. After I came up from the last dunk, daddy said " ok let's start making our way around guys." Everyone shouted "ok!" we grabbed our towels dried off a bit and headed down the walkway.

We passed a hotdog stand, and Gabriel asked if he could get a hot dog. "Sure honey" his mom said. "Andi, would you like a hot dog too baby?" daddy asked. "No daddy, I'm not hungry yet" I answered. "Ok baby let's walk a little slower so Gabriel can eat his hotdog before we get to the next set of adventures bet?" he asked. "Bet!" I responded and we bumped fists.

We walked slowly in front of them while he ate his packed hotdog. It had EVERYTHING on it! Cheese, ketchup, mustard and sour krout! Ugggh!!! Even though it was a lot of stuff it didn't take him long to eat it. He scarfed it. That's what daddy says people do when they eat too fast (giggles). Before we knew it we were ready for what was next up, the slippery carousel!

We got to the carousel and my dad asked Gabriel's mom to join me and he'd record for everyone. She agreed and the four of us walked through the gate. There was a lady standing right by the gate that told us where we should sit if we wanted to be together. Gabriel's mom asked us if we wanted to sit together or if we wanted to ride two separate ponies or if we wanted to have everyone sit together in the big moving car. We chose to sit together. We walked over to the car and Gabriel's dad helped everyone else get in before he did. First me, then

Gabriel's mom, then Gabriel. His mom buckled both our seatbelts and then her own. His dad sat across from us so he could take pictures and videos too. After all the people got on, there was one bell, then another. Slowly, the car started moving. I leaned over to Gabriel and whispered, "hey after this let's go to the lazy river, I've got a question to ask you." "Ok" he replied. Yes! I'm actually going to find out why I'm different!

Just then the car started to go faster, and with every circle the speed went up and we got sprayed with water. We screamed with excitement and grabbed each other's hands. We went around and around, got splashed and splashed and loved it all. When the ride stopped, someone came on the loudspeaker and said that everyone should remain seated for 2-3 minutes to settle our bodies, because we may still be dizzy. Just then Gabriel unbuckled his seatbelt and shouted, "not me, I'm perfectly fine!" His mom and I chuckled and shook our heads. His dad tapped his shoulder and said, "you sure buddy?" "Yes, I don't need a minute, I'm ready to go now!" We all looked at each other and laughed. His mom unbuckled her seatbelt, then mine. His dad waited for us to help us down off the ride. Once everyone was off, we headed for the gate. Just as Gabriel got to the gate, he grabbed hold of his stomach and yelled "mommy my tummy! I don't feel so good." She walked over to us quickly and asked, "what's wrong baby, tell mommy what you feel?" Before he could even get the words out, sour krout and cheese was all over him, his mom's shoes and the ground! He was really sick.

His dad grabbed him and ran to the nearest bathroom, but he couldn't get there fast enough. With every step he threw up some more. Me, my dad and his mom looked on in horror. My dad went and grabbed some tissues from a nearby stand so his mom could clean her shoes. We were all stuck just waiting for them to come out. We waited for what seemed like forever and then finally we saw them come out. Gabriel looked so sick and tired he could barely walk. He took two steps, and his dad lifted him up. Once they got over to us, his dad "hunny, let's call it a day. I think he is done for the day." She shook her head and said "yes, I agree. We should get him home." They both looked at my dad and I with the saddest faces and said "sorry guys to cut the fun short, but Mr. I'm ready now needs a bed." I walked over to him and touched Gabriel's foot. He opened his eyes and looked at me and I said "I'm sorry you feel sick Gabriel, I hope you feel better soon." He nodded once and closed his eyes back.

My dad gave his mom a hug and shook his dad's hand. Then, rubbed Gabriel's back and said "get better soon buddy. We'll have a longer time next time." This time he didn't open his eyes. He was fast asleep. Daddy grabbed my hand and lifted me up and we stood and watched as they walked away. I was sad. Not only was my friend sick, now I can't ask him about being different.

By the look on my face daddy knew I was upset. He kissed my cheek and said "hey wanna back to the fun, or did you have enough for the day?" Normally, nothing would get me out of Archer's Place. I'd wanna stay until I'm exhausted, but not this time. This time I just really wanna go home. "I had enough daddy, we can go now" I said. He rubbed my cheek and said "you sure cheeky? I know you're sad about Gabriel, but this is still your day." "I know, but I'm hungry and I wanna take a nap" I replied. "Ok then let's get our things, change into dry clothes and head out" he replied.

He put me down, held my hand and we walked back to the lockers. Once we got there he opened our locker and pulled the bags out. While he did that, I started removing my goggles and swim cap. Everything was out the locker and he closed it in. he grabbed the bags and picked me up and we headed for the family bathroom. That bathroom is cool, it's so that everyone can feel comfortable. Dads don't have to go into the women's bathroom with there daughters and moms don't have to go into the men's bathroom with their sons.

We got into the bathroom and daddy helped me get out of my bathing suit, dry off again and get into my clothes. Then I turned around to face the wall so he could get dressed. It was all pretty quick. We left the bathroom and was heading back to the car when daddy asked, "you don't wanna take a ty home baby?" "No daddy, I just wanna go" I replied. "Ok princess" he said. As we walked toward the exit, the same lady that gave us the bands coming in stood at the gate that we were headed out of. "Hey princess" she said while waiving at me. I looked at her and gave the best smile I could come up with and replied "hi." She could tell something was wrong. She walked over to us and said "hello beautiful, did you have a good time a Archer's Place today?" "Yes," I replied. She looked at me and then looked at my dad. She shook her head at him and asked if everything was ok. He told her that I was having a great time until my friend got sick and had to leave. "Ahhhh" she said. "I'm sorry your buddy got sick angel. Sometimes hanging here is great when you have a friend right?" "Yes" I replied. She was right, but I was ok when I thought it was just me and daddy.

Gabriel gave me hope. Now he's no help either. When will I find out why I'm so different (I thought to myself)?

Daddy grabbed my hand and said "say bye to the nice lady cheeky." "Bye" I said. "Take care sweetheart, I hope next time is a much better experience. I look forward to seeing you again" she said. "Ok" I replied, and we walked off. We got to the car, daddy let me in first and then put the bags back in the trunk. I was all buckled up and ready to go. Daddy got in the car and reached to open the small door for my tablet. Before he could take it out, I said "no, it's ok daddy. I'll probably fall asleep." "You sure baby?" he replied. "Yes I'm sure, I just wanna ride." He looked at me through the driving mirror, closed back the door and put the address in the gps. He put his seatbelt on, plugged his phone up and pressed the screen to hit start. The gps lady said "you should reach your destination by 2:25pm." I looked at the clock on the front of the car and it was 1:40.

As we drove out to the street, I saw kids with adults. Some of them looked just alike, some of them not so much. I wondered if they cared, if they felt like they were different, and how they came into the world. While driving, I saw things I normally don't see when we're coming. There was a diner right outside of the park that I had never seen. When did that get there? Was it always there? Did I just not

know? I wanted to ask daddy but I didn't really wanna talk. We kept

driving and there were houses I had never seen, and a farm! When did

they put a farm here? How come I never saw any of this before? Did

daddy know? We came to Archer's Place a brunch of times and I never

saw this stuff! Was it because I'm always sleeping, or did I just not pay

attention? I guess I was so focused on where I wanted to go, I couldn't

see anything else.

Even though I didn't wanna talk, I wanted to know about these

things. "Daddy" I said. "Yes baby" he replied. "Did you know there

was a diner back there?" "Yes cheeky, it's always been there" he said.

"And did you know there was a farm and houses too?" I asked. "Yes,

my love those have been there the whole time too" he chuckled.

"Hmmmm how come I never knew?" I asked. "Well baby, you didn't

wanna let me know" he said. "Huh?" I replied. "Yes baby, but it

happens to everyone even grown-ups. Sometimes we get so busy

thinking about the one thing we want or are focused on, that we forget

to take notice of all the other great things around us as well." "You

know what they call this baby?" he asked. "No daddy" I answered.

"That's called being present" he said. "What does present mean?" I asked. He said "being present is about recognizing what's right here and right now. You see it's ok to want something and get excited about it, but sometimes we miss out on the cool stuff like that diner that makes Shisho shaped blueberry pancakes and the farm that has a Railey barn house because you're only interested in the park.

I couldn't believe what he was saying. I was really missing all this!? I wonder if I missed anything else. We drove a little further and then I heard the gps lady say "you've reached your destination." We weren't home, we were at my favorite restaurant! I smiled and looked at daddy through the driving mirror, and there he was smiling back at me. Daddy parked the car, unhooked his seatbelt and came out. He opened my door, helped me out and locked up. We walked across the street, and there was the sign. A big chicken wing (lol). Every time I see it I laugh. How could that be the sign of a restaurant? The food is so good. We usually sit at a big table with a lot of other people. A man, I think he's Chinese stays in the middle of it and cooks. It's so fun! He cooks all the food with these long flat things and can flip it in the air and into your mouth! Then, he gets his squirt bottle and squirts juice in people's mouths. It's so much fun!

We got into the restaurant and the lady at the counter gave us a fork and spoon wrapped in a napkin then took us to our seats. We are sitting right in the middle! That means he might squirt juice in my mouth! There was a family sitting right next to us, so we didn't sit right away. Daddy tapped the man on his shoulder and asked him to watch our seats so we could wash our hands. He shook his head and said "sure man, you and the princess take your time." We walked toward the bathroom and knocked on the door. No one answered so we went in. We each took turns washing our hands and drying them. Daddy used the tissue to open the door and we left out to head back to our seats. He loves this restaurant just as much as I do because the food is good, but also because it has the family room.

When we got back to our seats daddy said thank to the man and we sat. There were plates in front of us and the cook guy started the show. He made rice, then chicken and flipped and turned all the food upside down. He had the juice squirter right next to him, and just then he looked at me. My eyes got wide with excitement. He looked right at me and smiled. He pointed at me and then the juice, I shook my head yes. Daddy looked at me and said "cheeky you ready? He's coming to you!" I replied "yup!" The Cookman picked up the juice squirter and got a little closer to us. He started yelling "hey hey" and everyone

yelled it back and started to clap. He pointed at me, raised the juice

squirter and pressed. I tilted my head back, opened my mouth and just

like that I was swallowing the juice. I couldn't believe it! I laughed and

some juice came out of my mouth. Daddy laughed, hugged me and

kissed my forehead. I was in heaven! We ate and talked, and when we

were done, we left a tip and walked back to the car.

After getting back on the road, it didn't take us long to get

home. When we got in the car the time was 4:32 pm. Daddy pulled into

the garage at 5:27pm. Believe it or not, I'm pooped! Daddy usually says

that anything after 2 pm is too late for a nap. So, I'll just take a bath

and read 2 books until I fall asleep.

We got in the house, hung the wet clothes, put all the stuff away

and I got ready for a bath. I stayed in there until I was wrinkled. When

I got out, daddy had my pajamas on the bed with the lotion and 2 books.

I dried myself off, lotioned up and put my pajamas on. After that, I

called him in so we could read together. I read my favorite book to him

"The girl that stood out) and he read his favorite book to me (There's

no such thing as too much love). I could barely get through the last few

pages of his book. I asked him what time it was and said "it's 8:47

cheeky." I rubbed his hand and said "bedtime?" He replied, "bedtime baby." We got in position to say our prayers and began. "Now I lay me down to sleep, I pray the lord my soul to keep, if I should go before I wake, I pray the lord my soul to take." He helped me back into bed, pulled the covers up to my chest and kissed me on the forehead and said "I love you so very much cheeky." "I love you too daddy" I replied. "Have a good night's rest baby, tomorrow we are gonna go see Grandma Jamie" he said. I smiled, shook my head yes, and off to lala land I went.

Riiiing riiiing riiing the telephone rang. I popped open my eyes and heard talking. I turned my head to the wall and looked at the clock, the time was 11:00 am. 11:00! The sun is out! Daddy never let's me sleep this late! What's going on? I pulled the covers back, turned and hopped off the bed. My slippers are so fuzzy and cute, but they make my feet hot, so I just grabbed my house socks in the drawer.

As I walk toward the door, I heard him say "I don't know what to say ma, I wasn't prepared to talk about this so soon." I kept walking out and saw him in the kitchen pacing back and forthwith such a worried look on his face. "Morning daddy" I said calmly. "Morning princess" he said. He looked at me and smiled and motioned for me to go brush my teeth. I smiled back and gave him a thumbs up. I went into the bathroom, got my stool for the sink, opened the medicine cabinet and got all the things I needed out. "Toothbrush check!" "Toothpaste check!" "Mouthwash check!" "Face rag missing!" Hmmm I can't do my morning stuff without my face rag. How am I going to wash my face? I came down off the stool and went to head back to the kitchen. Daddy was still on the phone.

Just then I heard him say "I should pick Mariela up, so they can hang out today. She hasn't had much luck with her friends this weekend." My eyes lit up! Mariela is my cousin. We used to see each other all the time but her dad took her to his house when her mom got really sick. Her mom and my dad are brother and sister; but my dad never let me go to their house, so Mariela was always at mine. Right before Aunt Marcy went to sleep forever, her and daddy had a big fight. He told Grandma Jamie that he went to her house, and she was putting that stuff in her arms again.

I don't know what the big deal was, if she's sick shouldn't she give herself medicine? She would always ask daddy for $5 to help her get medicine. But, no matter who she asked they would always tell her no. why would anyone want somebody to feel sick and be in pain? If I had money, I would give it to her. Last year we didn't hear from her for a while, daddy and grandma went looking for her and Mariela when they came back, they only had Mariela. She came into my room, but she was really sad. She said her mom was really sick and sleeping for 2 days. She was taking her medicine and fell asleep. She never woke up again.

I hope she's not still sad like she was that day. I miss her and I don't wanna be sad. Maybe since her mom isn't here anymore, she thinks she's different too. Maybe she knows why I'm different. That's it! Mariela is gonna help me find out. Just then daddy looked at me and said "what's up cheeky?" I told him I didn't have a face rag. He said, "ok go get started, I'll bring it to you once I turn the fire off." "Ok" I replied. As I started to walk back to the bathroom daddy says, "hey bacon, eggs, strawberries?" I smiled and said, "sure if that's all you got," we both laughed.

I went back into the bathroom and started brushing my teeth. Just as I went to pour the mouthwash in my morning cup, daddy walked in with my rag. "Here cheeky, make sure you hurry up in here. I wanna eat breakfast and head out to grandma's before 2'oclock." "Ok, I'll be right out." Once I was done, I went back into the kitchen and sat at the table. He brought the pan over and put some eggs, bacon, and a bowl of strawberries in front of me. This is my favorite breakfast, but I love it most when he makes it. He put the same in his plate but he like blueberries, YUCK! While we were eating, he said "hey cheeky, guess who else will be at Grandma Jamie's today?" "Who?" I replied (even though I already knew). "Mariela" he said. I smiled so hard you could barely see my eyes.

He laughed and said "I guess we should get going huh?" I nodded my head yes and ate my last strawberry. I hopped off the chair , put my stuff in the sink and went back to the bathroom to take my shower. He came in right after me, turned on the water, handed me the wash rag and helped me into the shower. I'm a big girl so I can shower alone. I call him in when I'm done to do one last wash and then I get out.

Since we had to hurry up I did it all by myself. When I got out of the shower, I dried off and went straight into the room. Daddy had already laid my clothes out on the bed. A blue and white adidas track suit. I lotioned my skin, put on my underwear, and when I was completely dressed, I went to daddy's room. "Daddy I'm dressed" I said. "Ok cheeks, I am too. Let me grab my keys and wallet and I'll meet you at the door" he said. "Ok" I replied and headed to the door. I walked over to the shoe rack and grabbed my blue adidas sneakers. Daddy met me there and he had on his red and white adidas track suit I looked at him and smiled. He started laughing. "What is it cheeky?" he asked. "Oh nothing, I just noticed how much you wanna dress like me" I said. He held his stomach and laughed. "IIIIII want to dress like you?" he asked. "Yes! You love me and you want to be my twin and that's ok!" I said. He kept laughing wile pulling out his red adidas sneakers. When he was all laced up and completely ready, he stood in the mirror fixing his jacket and then grabbed his phone. I pretended not to look but started counting down in in my head. He's gonna say come here cheeky let's take a selfie in 5,4,3,2. "Hey come here cheeky let's take a selfie." I just bust out laughing. "Now what?" he asks. "Oh, nothing daddy I just knew this would take a while that's all" I replied. "Is that so?" he asked. "Yes sir" I replied while fixing my jacket and preparing to take the picture. "Ok, we will only take 2 pictures" he said. "Suuuure we will" I replied. "No really, that's all we have time for" he said. He bent down and kissed my cheek for the first one and then we both turned to the side facing the mirror with one foot out for the second.

Both or them were actually pretty cool. Normally we take about 5 or 6 because something wasn't right the last time. He swiped through both pictures and asked me what I thought. "Eh look cool next to me" I said holding back my smile. He looked me straight in the eye and we both started laughing. "Ok miss, that's fine let's go" he said. He got his keys and wallet, and we walked out the door. We got to the elevator he grabbed some mints, I pressed the button and we waited. Before the elevator came, I grabbed his hand and looked up at him. "I love you daddy" I said. "Thank you baby. I love you too. Wow! What did I do to get that?" he asked. I shrugged my shoulders and said "I don't remember if I said it yesterday, so I don't wanna miss today." Daddy always says that we should take every opportunity to tell people you love them because you never know when will be the last time you see them, or that they just may need to hear it in a moment. He grabbed me close and rubbed my ear lobe. That was how he let me know he was being "sappy," you know without all the sap.

The doors opened and we got on. We got to the ground floor and turned left to head to the garage. Daddy stopped and waived at the desk. When I looked it was just Terry. Terry waved at me, and I waved back, and daddy and I went on toward the garage. He put the code in, opened the door and we walked toward the car. He unlocked the doors, opened my side and helped me in. It's the same routine all the time. I go into my seat buckle up and wait for him to get in and hand me my tablet and headphones. He opened his car door, got in, got my tablet and headphones out and handed it to me then started the car. While I swiped through to see what game I wanted to play, daddy buckled his seatbelt, waited for his phone to connect to the car and then searched for his favorite playlist (Def Jazz) *shrugs*. He says those were the jams back in the days and now they are jazz songs. It's cool, I guess. He makes me bop along and tell him I like it from time to time. Actually, I kinda like it but I won't tell him that.

Once it started, he looked in the driving mirror, gave me a thumbs up, I gave him a yes nod and we pulled off. When we got to the front of the garage we stopped. Daddy rolled down the window and started talking, it was Jaxon. He was cleaning the front of the building. He walked over to the car and spoke to daddy, then looked in the backseat and said, "why hello there princess Andi, how do you do today?" I smiled and said " hi Jaxon, I'm good thank you." He replied, "headed out to hang out with dad on the town huh?" "No, we're going to see my grandma" I said. "Ahh is that the pretty Grandma Jamie?" he asked. "Yes!" I replied. "Great, well I won't hold you guys back anymore. You tell Grandma Jamie I said hello, ok?" he said. "Ok" I replied, and he walked back to the building. Daddy rolled back up the window and we started to drive again. I looked over at the clock and it was 1:22pm and I pressed start on my game. Just as I got to level 6, I felt a tap on my shoe. I looked up and moved one side of the headphones from my ear. "We're here cheeky, let's go" daddy said. "Ok daddy" I replied. I stopped the game, handed him the tablet and headphones and unbuckled my seatbelt.

I waited for him to put it away and get out so he could come get me. Just then he turned to me and said "hey wanna wake your tablet with you and play games with Mariela?" With full excitement in my eyes, I said "yes! I have a new game I wanna show her." "Ok" he replied. He handed me back the tablet, put the headphones away and got out of the car. He came over to my door, opened it up and helped me out. Afterwards, he closed the door, pressed the button to lock the door and grabbed my hand. He looked at me, looked at the street and then spun me around 3 times. I got dizzy and yelled out "daddy! Ok ok!" "Wellll you know what to do right?" he asked. "Yes!" I replied and made my way to the other side of him.

Daddy says girls and ladies should always walk on the inside of boys and men so that they can protect us; and, because it is the gentlemanly thing to do. Anytime I'm on the outside of him, he spins me around until I get to the right side of him. We started walking and passed building 1014. Grandma Jamie lives in building 1016. Her address is 1016 Jackson Avenue. That's why her and Jaxon get along so well. Jaxon always says she lives on his street. When we got to the building, I asked daddy if I could press the bell. "Go ahead baby" he replied. I looked for her apartment number, its 4J. I pressed it and counted to 3, that's how daddy taught me. About five seconds later we heard "who is it?" and I yelled "it's me Grandma Jamie, Andi!" "Ok" she replied, and the door buzzed. We walked to the elevator, got up to her floor and daddy used the latchy thing by the eye hole to knock the door. When she opened the door, her eyes lit up and I screamed "hi grandma!" "Hi my sugarplum" she said.

She grabbed me and gave me 100 kisses and we went inside and took off our shoes and jackets at the door. I headed straight to the bathroom to wash my hands. When I came out, daddy went in and I went into his old room (the room that's mine now but shhh). I put my tablet down and grabbed my slippers then went back into the living room. Just as I went to sit on Grandma's lap, the doorbell rang. Grandma looked at daddy and said, "baby see who that is please." "Yes ma" he replied. Daddy walked over to the door and pressed the speaker button thingy and said "who?" "Its Kenny and Mariela" Uncle Kenny said. I was so excited I hopped off grandma's lap and went over to the door. I couldn't wait to see her. Daddy opened the door and we waited to hear the elevator open. We finally heard it, and then heard Uncle Kenny say, "Mari baby someone special is here to see you." "For real papi?" she asked. "Mhhm real special" he replied. As they got closer my smile got wider and wider.

Once Mariela spotted daddy she started running toward the door. It's almost like she didn't see me. At first, I was confused. Is the surprise really daddy? Did she not see me? She ran straight to daddy screaming "uncle, uncle, I missed you!" "I missed you too Mari baby, did you see your surprise?" he asked while pointing at me. She looked over and let out the biggest scream ever while wiggling her way out of his arms. "Andi! Andi! Andiiiiiii!" She just kept screaming my name. I was confused. Didn't she see me? Even though I didn't understand, I was still excited. "Hi Mari!" I yelled. We hugged and jumped, hugged and jumped. Daddy and Uncle Kenny stood at the door watching us and laughing, while Grandma waited for us to come give her some love. Daddy and Uncle Kenny shook hands then hugged. Daddy pulled Uncle Kenny in strong and shut the door.

Mari and Uncle Kenny took their shoes off at the door and right before we ran off, Uncle Kenny reached in his coat pocket and pulled out a case. He called Mari back "Mari baby come take your glasses." "Coming daddy" she said and grabbed the case. I waited there for her and took her hand and we ran into the room. When we got inside the room, we looked at each other and hugged and screamed again. I looked at her and said "wait, I have a new game to show you." I ran back into the living room grabbed my tablet off the couch and ran straight back in the room. "Careful Andi" daddy yelled. "Ok!" I yelled back.

I pressed the power button on the side, and we waited for it to turn on. While we waited, I turned to her and said "hey, you can't see?" She laughed and said "of course I can see, it's just sometimes I squint when things are small or too far away." I thought about when they got off the elevator, maybe that's why she saw daddy first. My tablet came on and the screen saver was two pictures side by side. One with me and mommy, and one with me and daddy. Mari looked at it and got sad.

She pushed herself back onto the bed and put her head on the wall. She put her head down. "What's wrong Mari?" I asked her. "I miss my mommy" she said. I got sad too. I just didn't know what to say. I would miss my mommy too if she never woke up again. So, I put the tablet down and pushed myself back on the wall to sit right next to her. I put my head on her shoulder and said, "I'm sorry Mari, I didn't mean to make you sad." She put her head on my head and said, "it's ok, I just miss her that's all." Just then grandma walked in with our favorite cookies and saw our faces. She put the cookies on the dresser and asked, "what's wrong with my girls?" As soon as she touched our hands, Mariela started crying "I miss my mommy." I felt so bad for bringing the tablet upstairs. I should have just left it in the car.

Hearing her cry made me cry and I just started screaming "I'm sorry, I'm sorry, I'm so sorry." Grandma looked so sad. She grabbed us both and squeezed us. "Grandma is right here my babies, it's ok let it out, let it out" she said. I felt bad that I made Mari sad and even more bad that I'm crying while she's crying. I looked at grandma and said "grandma I shouldn't be sad, but I love her and I don't want her to be sad." She looked at me while rubbing Mari's back and said "it's ok baby when we love someone we don't wanna see them sad. Sometimes we feel their sadness even more because we don't know how to make them not be sad in the moment. The only thing we can do is hold on to them tight and let them know we are right here. Sometimes all they need is to know that we won't leave them in that moment." I shook my head and looked at Mari. I grabbed her neck and kissed her on the cheek and said "Mari, I won't leave you. It's ok that you're sad and I'm right here." She grabbed my stomach and hugged me even tighter. She looked at grandma and then looked at me and said, "thank you."

Grandma let us hug it out and said "I'm gonna carry the cookies back in the kitchen and I'll be right back. Maybe we'll let uncle Brian and uncle Kenny hang out and we take a nap in here." We both shook our head yes. Once she walked out, we heled each other and laid down. When grandma came back in the room this time she had a book and put it on the dresser. Mari was already sleeping, and I was still hugging her. Grandma looked at me and whispered "take a nap with your cousin baby. Do you need grandma to lay down with you?" I shook my head no because I didn't want her to stay. I wanted to hug Mari but if she left, who was gonna hug me? She looked at me with the softest eyes I ever saw and she said, "I think I should stay, I know you want to take care of Mari, but don't forget about you." I didn't really understand,

and she could tell. She said, "make room" and climbed in the bed behind me then held me like I held Mari.

She kissed my cheek and said softly "baby as you get older, you will always want to take care of people and that's ok. But always make room for someone to take care of you, ok?" " Ok grandma" I replied. She rubbed my cheek until I fell asleep. That's how I fell asleep as a baby. That's why daddy still calls me cheeky.

"You have to tell her at some point," I heard Uncle Kenny say. I popped open my eyes and looked around, and grandma was gone. Mari was still sleeping, so I stayed next to her. I heard grandma say "Kenny, this is no easy task but you are right. B the longer you wait, the more questions she'll have. She loves you son, that won't change." There was no talking for a little bit, then I heard daddy say "I've been so worried about if she'll understand, and if she'll love me. I forgot that we teach her daily how important it is that I love me. If I love me, it doesn't matter who doesn't love me, but those that do will love me hard and on purpose." I got sad and thought to myself. "Does daddy think I don't love him? How? He's my best friend. He is so funny and caring. He always talks things out with me and cooks me whatever I want. Everyone loves him, but not more than me. Now I'm confused. Am I different or is he?" I turned my head to the dresser and saw the book that grandma put there earlier. There were some papers sticking out of it. I stared at it forever, then I heard daddy say "you're right, she's my baby and she loves me. We will have the talk soon. It's getting late, let's get them up." I heard walking and I closed my eyes and pretended I was still sleeping. Daddy walked in the room and whispered "Andi, Mari, wake up girls, it's time to go home." I slowly opened my eyes and looked at him and said, "ok daddy." When I moved my arm from Mari, she turned and woke up. "Hey niecey, feeling better?" daddy asked. "Hi uncle, yes I feel better. Andi and grandma made me feel so much better" she replied. "Good baby, we're getting ready to go home so you girls get up and meet us in the living room" he said. He looked at me, smiled and said "bet?" "Bet" I replied with a smile.

Mari and I both sat up and looked around the room. Mari said that it had looked so different from when she was staying there. After her mom went to sleep, she stayed with grandma for two weeks because her dad was so sad. Grandma changed the room around a lot since then. We held hands and scooted to the edge of the bed. "Hey, on 3 we jump down" I said. She smiled and nodded "on 3" she replied. "1,2,3!" I yelled, and we both hopped off the bed. We laughed hard when we hit the ground, but grandma came running in the room in a panic. "Girls, girls, are you ok?" "Yes grandma" Mari replied. Grandma gave us this worried look, then upset, then laughed. We looked at each other and giggled. "Ma is everything ok in there?" daddy yelled. "Yes son, the girls were just having some fun" she replied. "Ok we're waiting for them at the door, tell them to come out" he replied. "Come on girls you heard him" she said as she helped us up and kissed our foreheads.

As we were walking out, I noticed a picture hanging out of the book that she brought in earlier. I don't know why, but I pulled it out really quickly and shoved it in my pocket. Once we were both out of the room, grandma turned the light off and followed us to the door. Daddy had my sneakers and jacket in his hands and Uncle Kenny had Mari's shoes in one hand and her jacket and glasses case in the other. I took my sneakers from daddy and put them on, then stood to the side and waited for Mari to get hers on.

When we had our shoes on, grandma said "I love you all so much, thank you for the wonderful visit today." Everyone at the same time said "we love you too." Each of us gave her a hug and walked out the door. Daddy was last. When he went to hug her, she looked at him and said "I love you, so does she remember that." He kissed her cheek and said "thanks ma for everything, I love you. Ill give you a call tomorrow." "Ok baby" she replied. Mari and Uncle Kenny had walked to the elevator; and, just as daddy turned to walk away from grandma the doors opened. "Come on Uncle Brian. Come on Andi" Mari yelled. "Coming" I yelled and we hurried up to get on. We got all the way downstairs when I realized that I didn't have my tablet. I tugged at daddy's hand and said, "daddy I'm sorry, I forgot my tablet upstairs." He looked at Uncle Kenny and said "you guys go ahead, we gotta go back up." "You sure you don't want us to wait?" Uncle Kenny asked. "No man we're good. We've both been waiting long enough to leave, go ahead" daddy replied. "Ok man, it was good seeing you as always and let's lock in next weekend for real" Uncle Kenny replied. "Got you brother" daddy replied, and they slapped five and hugged. Uncle Kenny kissed my forehead and Mari and I hugged again, then they walked out the building. Me and daddy turned around to walk back to the elevators and then we heard a ding. Grandma Jamie walked off the elevator. She smiled and handed me my tablet. "I believe someone forgot this upstairs. I wonder who it could be?" she asked. I smiled and took the tablet and hugged her tight. "Thanks grandma! You're the best!" I yelled. Daddy went in for another kiss too and said, "thanks ma, you didn't have to come down, we were gonna come up." "No worries baby, I needed to stretch my legs" she replied. They both laughed hard. She walked us to the front door and held it as we each walked out. I counted 1,2,3 cars before we got to our car. Like always, daddy unlocks the door, let's me in, you know the routine.

Once daddy was in the car, I was buckled in and he turned on some music, I handed him the tablet to put away. I was pretty exhausted with the day. He must've known, because he didn't ask me any questions. He just took it and put it away. "I love you so much cheeky" I heard him say. I looked up to the driving mirror and saw him staring at me. I smiled and said "I love you so much too daddy." He winked at me and then we started to drive. I put my head back and just stared out the window.

Although I was tired, I didn't fall asleep. I kept replaying the day and asking myself a ton of questions that I couldn't answer. Will Mariela ever actually see her mommy again? Will she always cry when she sees me with my mommy? Will I always have to hold her to sleep when she cries? What if I'm sad and she's sad at the same time? I never did get to ask her if she knows why I'm different, when do I see her again? Is daddy really ready to tell me? I think grandma and Uncle

Kenny know, why didn't I ask them? Over and over the same questions were in my mind with no answers. Suddenly, we stopped and when I looked up, we were in the garage. I didn't even know we were already back at the house.

Daddy blew a kiss at me, and I blew one back. "You ready to head up cheeky?" he asked. "Yup all ready" I replied. I unbuckled my seatbelt and waited for him to open my door. Once the door was open, he stretched for my hand, and I hopped out. "Soon you're just gonna put one foot on the ground and step out. You're getting so tall" he said. "Ill be taller than you in a few years" I chuckled. He looked at me with serious eyes and we stared at each other. Five seconds later we both started laughing. Daddy's a little on the short side but shhhh don't tell him that. He thinks he's taller than everyone he knows. He kissed me on the forehead, shut the door behind me and pressed the button to lock the car.

While we walked to the door to get into the building, I heard a voice say, "Hey Mr. Brian, hey Andi." It was Cameron. Cameron and his mom lived three doors down from daddy. "Hello Cam and Ms. Brown" we both said. They're really nice, and sometimes when Malia comes over on Saturday, Cameron comes over too. He doesn't have a dad, just his mom, grandparents, and two uncles. One time Cameron and his mom came over and when I went to the bathroom, I overheard his mom say "I couldn't wait any longer for the man of my dreams. I was 41 and wanted a baby." I don't really know what she meant by that, but Cameron never had a dad, and when I asked him about it, he said "sometimes I wish I had a dad cuz all the other kids have a dad. Even another mom would be okay because then I'd have two parents like some of the other kids. But mommy always tell me I'm special and I kinda like the sound of that, so I guess it's ok."

Hmmm, maybe I should've started with Cameron. I'll ask daddy if he can come over next weekend. We all walked into the door. While we waited on the elevator, daddy spoke to Ms. Brown and Cameron showed me his new game. When the doors opened, daddy told Cameron to stand aside and let me and Ms. Brown on because ladies go first. When we were all on the elevator Cameron asked his mom if he could press the button to our floor. She said "go ahead baby, you know where we're going." He pressed for the seventh floor, and they slapped high five.

We all got off the elevator and walked down the hallway. When they stopped at their door, me and daddy said goodnight to them and kept going. Even though it wasn't extremely late, I felt really tired. Once we got inside we took our shoes off, daddy was already holding our jackets and he put them on the hooks. I walked toward my room and daddy said "take your clothes off cheeky. Get ready for a quick shower school tomorrow." "Ok daddy" I said and did just that. I got undressed, put my robe on and went into the bathroom.

By the time I got in there, daddy was in there getting the water right. I put my hand in to feel the water and it was just right. He looked at me and asked, "good princess?" I gave him the thumbs up and said, "it's perfect sir!" He laughed and walked toward the door and pulled the door just a little bit. I took off my robe and got in the tub. Face, neck, underarm, belly button, special place, backpack! I got all the essentials. My happy place is in the water, but I'm sleepy so no long bath tonight. I rinsed off twice and then turned off the water. I put one foot out and leaned over to grab my towel and started drying off one foot at a time like mommy taught me. I put my robe back on, slid on my slippers and went into my room. I closed the door behind me and went over to the bed.

Daddy knocked the door and I heard "cheeky let me know when you're all done so we can say prayers." "Ok daddy" I said. I opened up the top drawer and got some underwear out and then pulled the bottom drawer open and grabbed my favorite red and white pajamas. I grabbed the lotion off the dresser and took everything back over to the bed. I got lotioned up, put my clothes on, hung up my robe and called daddy back to the room "ready daddy" "coming cheeky" he said. I turned and walked back to the bed.

By the time I got back he was walking through the door. He stretched his hand to me, and I grabbed his. We both kneeled down at the edge of the bed. He kissed the back of my hand, and then my forehead. "Who's the most beautiful baby girl in the whole wide world?" he asked. "Me!" I said. "You know it" he said. "And who is the most luckiest daddy in the world?" I asked. He laughed and said, "I am certain that's me!" We both chuckled and bowed our heads and closed our eyes.

I began to say our prayer "now I lay me down to sleep I pray the Lord my soul to keep. If I should go before I wake, I pray the Lord my soul to take." Then daddy started his right after "to our beloved most high, we give thanks for today, we give thanks for tonight and for the opportunity to be safe in our home. We ask that you protect us in it, our family and friends in their home, and share a special blanket of comfort, peace and protection over strangers, the homeless and those going through physical and mental distress. We thank you for all good things, for all things that serve as a lesson and for the growing love we share. In your highest honor we pray and say Amen!" "Amen!" I said.

We both got up and I climbed into bed. He pulled the covers up halfway just like I like it and said "I love you so so much cheeky, good night." "I love you too daddy, good night" I said. He bent over the dresser and turned my night light one. I grabbed my sleepy pillow, turned on my side and watched him walk out. I was sleeping before I saw pull the door in.

"Andi, Andi mama" I heard daddy calling out to me. I opened my eyes just enough to make eye contact, but not fully wide. "Good morning sleepyhead" he said. "Good morning daddy" I replied. He opened his arms for a hug and slowly I got up. I got out of the covers and opened my arms. Daddy scooped me up and started kissing me all over my forehead and face. I laughed and squirmed because it tickled so much. "Daddy! Stop!" I yelled while giggling. "I just need to make sure that princess Andi is awake that's all" he said. "I'm awake! I'm awake!" I yelled while grabbing his face. "Ok beautiful, breakfast is ready when you are. Get your slippers on and come out to the kitchen so you can hop in the bathroom, and we can head out" he said. "Ok daddy, coming" I said.

He likes when I brush first, then eat. But I told him that I like to eat first then brush because brushing first makes my food taste weird. Every now and again he lets me do things my way. I put my slippers on and went to the kitchen. I could smell my favorite! Yes! Turkey bacon and honey biscuits! He really does love me. I pulled the stool away from the counter a little bit and climbed on. I was smiling at breakfast so hard I didn't see him smiling at me. When I looked up and saw him, I chuckled. "I really do love you baby!" he said. "I love you too big guy!" I said. "It's 6:47 baby, we are really early but remember this week is rehearsal for the show" he said. "I remember pop" I replied.

Next week my school is having a show. It's so exciting! My class is doing a play called **I like being different**. We all have different parts and some of us have some special parts and we can talk about ourselves being different. Malia and Gabriel already know why they're different, but I still don't know (sigh). Maybe I should tell Ms. Monty I don't need a special part. I don't really have anything special to say. Ms. Monty is my favorite teacher. She says kids teased her when she was growing up because she was different than them. She said that she thought she was a normal kid until she got to third grade and the kids started making fun of her. Her skin is orangey-brown, and she has freckles and orangey hair. She lived with her grandma because her parents played instruments in a band and they couldn't take her everywhere.

The kids teased her because of how she looked and they kept telling her she didn't have any parents. Her grandma complained to the school and then one day she put her in a different school. Every morning she started saying sentences over and over that Ms. Monty would say in the mirror. She said it helped her feel better. So now we all do it at home and in school. She calls it a mantra. Ms. Monty says "everyone is unique, and was made especially in their own way and is just as important as the person standing next to you no matter how different they are from each other." She says really nice things to make us feel good but she really gives the best hugs.

"You finish eating cheeky?" I heard daddy say. I had one more piece of bacon and one bite of biscuit left. "Almost big guy" I replied. "Ok, I'll turn the shower on, put your plate in the sink and head in" he said. "Yes sir!" I replied. I ate my last bites, hopped down off the stool and put my plate in the sink. I took a few sips of tea because it's cooled now and put that in the sink too. I went into the room and grabbed my robe. I turned my head quickly to the closet and saw the picture I took from Grandma Jamie's house on the floor by the curtain where my clothes were folded up.

I ran quickly and picked it up and stuffed it in between a book in my bag. I was so nervous, I didn't want daddy to know I took it. Daddy always says, "you don't take anything from anywhere and anyone that wasn't given to you." I felt bad for taking it, but I just wanted to see what kinds of pictures were in the book and we didn't have much time last night. It's probably an old picture of Grandma Jamie and grandpa Sedwick. I never met him. He went to sleep before I was born. "Come on baby, I wanna get going" daddy yelled out. I hopped up, zipped up my bag and ran to the bathroom. "Here I am daddy" I said. "Ok cheeky hop in, I'm gonna iron our clothes" he said. "Ok" I cheered. He put his hand up for a high five. I slapped it and said, "I'm out!" he walked out and pulled the door in just a bit.

I got undressed and got in the shower. I started to say my mantra "I am fearless, kind, honest, and strong. Even on my bad days, I know nothing went wrong. Impossible is nothing and perfection is a myth. Love is greater than hate, so that's what I lead with!" Ms. Monty likes us to say our mantras in the mirror, she says its important that we know exactly who we are speaking to when we say them. I like to say it in the shower too. So, I have two. The first one I say in the shower, that's the one daddy helped me with. The other one I say in the mirror is what I came up with for our class project last month. They make me smile and when I'm sad it makes me happy again. I said my shower mantra one more time and turned the water off. When I say it two times, that's enough for my morning shower. Me and daddy worked that out a little while ago.

I dried my skin and went over to the sink to brush my teeth. Daddy had it all laid out for me. Toothbrush, toothpaste, mouthwash, flossy pick. I did my routine, grabbed my robe and was ready to head back in the room. As I opened the door I saw daddy walk from my room to his room and he yelled "good job cheeky, two mantras like we practiced." I smiled and said, "yup just like we practiced!" I walked into my room and slightly shut the door. When I walked over to the bed, I saw my clothes laid out on the bed. Everything, except my underwear. He usually let's me pick that on my own. I walked over to the dresser, opened my top drawer, grabbed a pair of panties, an undershirt and a pair of school socks. On top of the dresser was my lotion, my lip gloss tray and my jewelry box. I grabbed my lotion and went over to the bed. I dropped everything on the bed and sat down. Usually, I would say write five things I'm grateful for while I lotion my skin, but since we trying to head out quickly, but we really don't have time.

I lotioned up and when I had my underclothes on, I took my pants over to the mirror behind the door to say my second mantra "I am beautiful an my smile is bright, no matter who is dim around me I will shine my light. I treat others with respect and honor myself because we all need each other we can't do it by ourselves. I consider others but don't leave myself out, and when things go off course I simply re-route. Yesterday is gone, so I won't get stuck there. Tomorrow hasn't come yet, but today is right here. We got this!" I smiled at myself in the mirror and said "I love you Andi!" Daddy says to truly understand love, we should start with ourselves. I walked back to the bed and put my school shirt on, then grabbed the lotion to put it back on the dresser.

I put the lotion back in it's place and grabbed my favorite lip gloss. I put a little on, rubbed my lips together and put the tube in my pocket. Afterwards, I walked back to the bed and picked up my robe and my book bag and went toward the door. I hung the robe on the hook, too one last look at myself in the mirror and went out the door. "Daddy I'm ready, I'm just gonna grab the brush for my hair, ok?" I yelled. "Great cheeky, I'll be out to brush it up in 2 minutes, ok?" he said. "Ok daddy" I replied. I walked into the bathroom, got my brush out of my cabinet, and put a little water on it so it can help smooth my hair back. Daddy has trouble when my curls are all over. He learned the water trick from mommy. I carried it out to the living room, and he walked out of his room. "You look beautiful cheeky" he said. "Thank you daddy, you're ok I guess" I replied. We looked at each other and laughed. He mushed my head and then grabbed it and kissed my forehead. We walked over to the couch, I sat down and turned on my side. After I handed him the brush, he started softly brushing my hair back. "Oh, cheeky you didn't forget to damp it, great job. Your daddy loves you" he said. I chuckled and said "I love you too daddy. You always say all this hair man! I can't handle all this hair." He laughed and replied "you're right, and that's why I love you." He kept brushing until all the sides were smooth and laid down. Then he took the hair tie from around his wrist and put my hair In a ponytail. I showed him how mommy did my buns and he did it! He really did it! And shhh don't tell mommy, but I liked his better.

I saw him smiling in the mirror next to the door and it made me smile too. "Ok Ms. Beauty pageant winner, up and out" he said. "Ok daddy! Hey thanks for the hairdo kid" replied. We looked at each other and started to laugh. He squeezed my cheeks and said "anything for you princess." I took the brush back to the bathroom and placed it in my cabinet and went back out to the living room. My bookbag, shoes and school sweater were all at the door ready to grab. I put on my shoes, then my sweater and then picked up my bag.

Daddy came over to the door, put his shoes on, picked up his bag and asked for a pinky of my lip gloss. I took it out of my pocket and squeezed some on his finger. He put it on his lips and said, "no more dry lips for us." "You mean for you?" I asked. We both laughed and he said, "ha ha ha very funny kiddo hit the door" he said. I gave him a wink and stood by the door. He turned off the lights and we walked out. When we got to the elevator, Cameron and his mom were coming out of their apartment. Every Monday daddy drops me to school and some days we see each other in the hallway. This Monday is different. Cameron has on the same school sweater as me! Huh? Did he change schools? What happened? I thought to myself.

"Good morning Ms. Brown, good morning, Cameron" I said. "Good morning neighbors!" daddy said at the same time. "Morning Andi, morning Mr. Brian!" Cameron said. "Morning neighbors, how is everyone?" Ms. Brown asked. Daddy said, "oh we're good thanks for asking." I just smiled. The elevator doors opened up and daddy stopped tot the side so everyone could get on and then he came in. I looked at Cameron and said "hey that's my school sweater, you're going to my school now?" "Yup, today's my first day!" he said. "That's so cool, now we can be school buddies too" I replied.

We both giggled and shook our heads. The elevator doors opened and daddy held the button for them to stay open until we all got off. Jaxn and Terry were both at the desk and yelled good morning to us and we all said, "Good morning!" As we walked to the garage door, I looked at Cameron and said "there's 3 third grade classes, we are all on the same floor and we go to lunch at the same time so we are definitely going to see each other." He smiled and his eyes got big. "I'm so happy I'll have at least one friend in this school! In my old school I didn't have any friends at all" he said with a sad face. I looked at him and said, "you do now!" He smiled wide.

Daddy grabbed my hand, and we went to the right. Ms. Brown grabbed Cameron's hand and they went to the left. "You guys have a wonderful day ahead. Oh hey Andi, today will be Cameron's first day at your school. Hopefully you guys see each other at some point, and you can show him the ropes" she said. "Sure, he's in good hands with me!" I replied. Ms. Brown and daddy both laughed. I didn't understand what was so funny. "See ya later Cameron" I said. "See ya later" he replied. "Ok tour guide hop in" daddy said as he opened the door. I gave him my bookbag, grabbed his hand and stepped into the car. He closed the door and walked around and opened the other car door to put my bookbag beside me. He winked at me and closed the door, then opened his and got in. He put his bag in the seat next to him and started the car.

The time showed 8:15. School starts at 8:50, and it's 11 minutes away. We are pretty early, but Ms. Monty wants us to come up to an hour early all week so we can get the play together. I'm excited for the show, but I still don't know what really makes me so special yet. "Cheeky, hey cheeky" I heard daddy calling me. "Yes daddy" I replied. "Hey I been calling you for a few seconds, you were in deep thought out the window. What were you thinking about?" he asked. "Oh nothing" I replied. He wasn't gonna tell me anyway, so I won't bother to ask. "You sure? You're looking a little sad and you know daddy doesn't like that" he said. "Yeah, I know, I'm ok" I responded.

I looked up at the driving mirror and daddy was staring back at me with a sad look on his face. It was like we both needed a hug. Two more right turns and we are at school. I turned my head back to my window and stared outside. We pulled up to the school, daddy got out and opened the back door on his side and got my bookbag out and closed the door behind him. He walked around the car to my door and opened it. "Awaiting princess Andi" daddy said with his hand stretched to me. I held his hand, hopped out and took my bookbag from him. "You don't want me to hold it until we get to the doors?" he asked. "No, I got it" I replied. He looked at me with a sad look and grabbed my hand. He didn't squeeze it, but he held it tight.

When we got to the doors, Ms. Eddy was standing there. Ms. Eddy is my principal. She is so sweet to all the kids, and she even knows us by name. She says we are all her babies, so she has to make sure we are getting the best out of our time at school. My dad and Ms. Eddy met on one of my school trips last year. Every time he sees her, he has this weird smile on his face. I don't know what that's all about but this morning things were different. "Good morning, Andi. Good morning, Mr. Brian" she said. "Good morning, Ms. Eddy" we both replied. I never looked up at her face. She stretched her hand down to mine and asked "hey, is everything ok baby? This isn't like you." "Yes Ms. Eddy I'm fine, I'm just gonna head to rehearsal" I replied.

I looked up at her and she looked over at daddy. They didn't say anything to each other but it was like they were talking with their eyes. I slid my hand out of hers and looked at daddy then waived. "See ya later dad" I said. "Hey cheeky come here" he said. I turned back and said "huh?" He stepped over to me and came down to kiss my forehead. He stood there for like ever. I rubbed his head and moved my head. He held my face and said "hey mom is gonna pick you up from school today. I may stop by later to see you. Cool?" "Sure, no problem" I said and walked away. I walked up the 2 steps and started to head down the hallway. At the end I made a right and the auditorium was at the other end. When I got there, I walked to the front by the stage and put my sweater and bag on one of the chairs.

"Morning Andi" everyone started yelling. "Good morning, everyone" I replied. "Good morning, Andi" Ms. Monty said. "Good morning, Ms. Monty" I replied. She walked over to me and asked "hey, it's almost play time, you ready?" "Sure" I replied. She looked at me and said, "baby girl is everything ok?" "Yes, Ms. Monty I'm fine" I replied. "Now I don't know if I should believe that since you haven't looked at me once" she said. I looked at her and thought to myself, maybe she doesn't know why but at least she cares about how I feel. I grabbed her hand and led her to a seat close to the stage. "Ms. Monty, this play is gonna be great! You worked so hard putting it together and some of us have some really special parts. All of us talk to each other about how exciting it is to have these parts in the play. The thing is everybody else already knows why they're so special and I'm the only one that doesn't. I asked my dad and all he ever says is that I'm not old enough to know. I guess, I guess I just don't feel like I shouldn't have a special part. Maybe you should give my part to someone else."

I looked at Ms. Monty and sat back in the chair. She rubbed my hand and then my face and then sat back in her chair too. She took a deep breath and started "you know Andi, one of the most important things we should never forget is that what makes us special is how different we are from one another. When you're surrounded by people that aren't like you it's the best time to learn. Some of us don't know all the small but important details and yet we still show up just as bright, charismatic and wholesome as we could ever be. You know what makes you special in my eyes?" she asked. I shook my head no. "May I share?" she asked. I shook my head yes.

"Every morning you get to school before most if not all of your classmates, so you can be first to greet everyone. You appointed yourself classroom monitor so you can stock up on the things that everyone needs. You remind me if I forget to do our daily mantras, anyone that's new to the class becomes your best friend and if you get something wrong you don't hide it, you tell the truth. All of those things have their own name from initiative, to intentionality, to accountability, to compassion. Most adults struggle with those things. With you it's so effortless, it's so natural, it's so special, it's so you. Sometimes it's not what we know or what we have that makes us special, it's who we are and how we make others feel too" she said.

She hugged me, and for that small moment everything felt right. She lifted my head up by my chin and said "baby girl, no matter the specifics your different is the type of different this world needs." I smiled and hugged her super hard. I felt better, I felt happier, I felt different! She squeezed my hand and kissed the back of it then let me go to get back to my classmates.

As she walked, she looked back and said, "when you're ready, we are." I asked, "can I just watch today?" She nodded yes, with a huge smile. I sat and watched everyone go over their parts and even though I knew it like the back of my hand, this time listening didn't feel the same. Although Malia has two moms, she is special to me because she's my best friend. She helped teach me how to ride my bike and make my first pancake. Every morning we race to see who could get to school first to set up each other's desk, and if either of us don't do so well on a test we help each other figure out where we got things wrong.

Gabriel is a different color from his parents, but he knows 4 different languages, and said he'd help me learn too. When we go to lunch, he picks one language and speaks to me in it the whole time until I start recognizing the words. He lived with two other families before his parents adopted him and no one knew English. He said it was hard at first but now everything is easy like English. Whenever a new kid comes to the school that speaks one of the languages he knows, he gets to skip class for the day to help them get settled. That's pretty cool. That's pretty special!

You know, the more I think about this, the better I feel. I am pretty special, and like Ms. Monty says "even if you don't know the specifics, what you know is special already." The bell rang, and that meant it was 8:45. We have five minutes to get to class. We lined up in double lines, stood next to our partners, and zipped our lips as we walked through the hallway to our class. When we got there, we took our books out of our bags and put the bags away. I held the book under my arm and walked toward my desk.

Just as I pass the first desk, BJ my friend that sits behind me called out to me and said "hey Andi, this fell out of your book." I looked down and my eyes opened wide. I took it from him and said, "thanks BJ." BJ has a lady that sits in the class with him Ms. Nora. She helps him understand the lessons a little bit slower because sometimes he has a hard time. He calls her his "para," she doesn't like that he feels bad about being the only one with extra help, so sometimes she comes to each of us and helps us with a math problem. He has a little trouble reading and sounding out words, so he gets shy. I heard Ms. Monty tell him one day that "autism isn't a disease, and he doesn't have to feel ashamed because of it." None of us really know what autism is but we all love BJ. He is an artist! He painted the big mural in the hallway and leads the art club when we all get good grades. He won the last two art awards for the school, and we got money to fix our playground. He is our HERO!

When I got to my seat, I flipped the picture over it was a picture of a lady. She was dressed like a boy, but I knew it was a lady. Who is this? She looks like my dad, but this isn't Aunt Marcy. Where did she come from? Does he have another sister I don't know about? How come I don't see her? I wonder if she's sleeping like Aunt Marcy. I have so many questions. "Hey Andi!" I heard Ms. Monty call out me. "Yes Ms. Monty" I replied. "Put that away please we are about to begin" she said. "Yes Ms. Monty" I replied. I put the picture in my pocket and opened my book.

Even though today is Monday, Ms. Monty says that since we've been working so hard this week and doing so good there will be a lot of surprises and relaxation this week.

After we all completed our morning work Ms. Monty said "today we are going to have lunch in the classroom. We are having a pizza party!" Everyone screamed! She laughed and asked us to help each other move the desks and chairs around. When we were done, she brought out a speaker and said "ok guys we're gonna have a little music but if we are gonna scream and jump, we can't. Dancing and laughing is fine but we are still in school. Deal?" "Deal!" we all said.

Just then there was a knock at the door. Ms. Monty went over to open it, and a table came rolling in. There were 3 pizza boxes, juice boxes, bottles of water, 4 big bags of chips and 2 boxes of fruit snack. All our eyes lit up. The table was almost all the way in when I saw my dad pushing it. I hopped up smiled so hard! It was as if I didn't just see him. I ran over to him and squeezed him so tight. "Hi cheeky" he said. "Hi daddy, what are you doing here?" I asked. "Well Ms. Monty told me she wanted to something special for you guys because you all have been working so hard so I asked if I could help" he said.

In a flash I thought about all the things Ms. Monty said made me special. These were all the things I worked on with my dad. I guess if I'm so special and he taught me, he has to be special too. But he is! He really is! He teaches me so many things, and is really funny. He cooks whatever I want and lays with me when I don't feel good. Whenever I don't know a word, he helps me figure it out, and he lets me say how I feel. Even though him and my mom don't live together, he's really nice to her and he always says she's the reason I'm his forever gift. He takes care of Grandma Jamie, and all his friends always call him with their stuff to talk about. My daddy is special! I guess I'm lucky too!

He hugged me tight and kissed my forehead, then started to help us set up for the party. While we were doing that, BJ came over to me and whispered "hey Andi, your dad is so cool. I wish my dad was like him." I looked at daddy and said, "he is and he's all mine." Everyone had a slice, snack and drink in front of them and we started to eat and talk. When most of us were done, Ms. Monty turned on the music and said "ok now let's burn this off." All of us got up and started to dance, even daddy. We danced and laughed, ate fruit snacks and drank water.

A little while later I saw daddy straightening up with Ms. Monty and I knew the party was almost over, but really he was just about to leave. He loaded the table back up with the empty boxes and garbage and headed toward the door. Before he walked out, he turned and waived at me to come to him. I walked over and grabbed his hand to walk out the door. He closed the door behind us and squeeeeezed my cheeks. "Did you have a good time at the party baby?" he asked. "Yup, I just wish you could stay" I said. He laughed and said "I know baby, I'd love to stay too but I ran away from work to be here and I have to get back. I will see you later today though, right?" "Yes" I said. "Ok good" he replied.

He kneeled down and hugged me tighter than ever before. I grabbed his face and just held it. He kissed me on my forehead and then my cheek, before he started to get up. As he stood up, I touched his hand and said "daddy, before you go can I ask you something?" "Sure cheeky, anything" he replied. "Did you have another sister?" I asked. "No cheeky, there was just me and Aunt Marcy you know that. Why do you ask?" he replied. "Yeah, I know, but I was confused when I saw this because she looks so much like you" I said. Just then I pulled the picture out of my pocket and gave it to him. He took it from me and his face got red. He looked at me and his eyes started to water. "Cheeky where did you get this?" he asked as the first tear fell. "I'm sorry daddy, I'm sorry, please don't cry. I saw it at grandma's house and I took it, but I didn't look at it until today. I'm sorry, please don't be sad or mad at me" I said as tears started rolling out of my eyes.

He turned and put his back against the wall, and slowly slid to the floor. He grabbed me and put me to sit on his lap. He looked at the picture, and then looked at me. I couldn't understand why he was crying, but him being sad made me sad. He rubbed my back and turned me toward him and said "cheeky, this is daddy." I was confused. I looked at him and then the picture and then I looked at him again. "No daddy, this is a girl. She has on boy clothes, but this is a girl. This isn't you" I said. "Yes baby I know, but this is daddy. It really is me" he said. "Are you a girl daddy?" I asked. "Not anymore cheeky, but I used to be and I'm sorry that I struggled to tell you before" he said. "Does this mean you are my mommy too? You're not my daddy anymore?" I asked. "No cheeky, all your life I've been your daddy. I was a girl long before you were born" he said.

I heard the door open, and Ms. Monty stepped out. She looked down at us and saw daddy holding the picture and she smiled. "Class is starting soon you two" she said and closed the door back. I looked at daddy and his head was down with tears running down his face. I really don't know what this means but it makes me so sad to see him sad. I hope he doesn't think I don't love him, he's my best friend. I picked his face up by his chin and asked him "are you gonna stop being my dad now?" "No baby, never! I'll be your dad until I'm not here anymore and even after that" he said. I hugged him and whispered in his ear "it sounds to me like you're different and what I learned is that different means special."

He held me and started to cry more. Then, he pulled me away from his chest and looked at me and said "how did I get so luck?" I smiled and shrugged my shoulders and said "I ask myself this all the time. How did my dad get so lucky?" We looked at each other and laughed. He stood me up and I took a napkin off the table and handed it to him. He wiped his eyes and blew his nose. I did the same with mine. He took my tissue from me and put them both in a pizza box. "Hey beautiful, you've got to get into class, daddy has to get back to work, ok?" he said. "Ok, will I still see you later?" I asked. "Of course mama" he replied.

We both took a deep breath and I walked into the class. As the door closed I turned and looked out the window and saw him walk with his head down. I opened the door, stepped out and said "hey." Daddy looked back and said "what is it baby?" I stretched for his hand and said "I like being different, it makes me special and you should too!" He smiled so bright and walked back and picked me up and squeezed me tight. "I love you sweet girl" he said. "I love you too big guy." He put me down and watched me walk back in.

I got to my desk just in time for "quiet time." During quiet time we write in our journals anything that's on our minds and how it makes us feel. This morning is journal entry #13:

Today I found out my dad used to be a girl. That's pretty strange. I didn't know girls could be boys. Does this mean boys can be girls too? I guess I'll ask him more questions later. Ms. Monty told me that sometimes the specifics don't matter. It's who we are and how we make people feel. I love my dad. He's special to me and he makes me feel like a princess. When I saw him cry, it made me cry because he is my best friend. It's ok that he's different, I am too and that makes us connected and special!

Ms. Monty walked over to me and rubbed my back. She read my page and a tear rolled down her face. "Are you ok Ms. Monty?" I whispered. "Yes Andi, I'm just happy that you realize how special you are" she said. "I know I'm special because I'm different and that's my favorite part" I replied.

I thought about all the questions I had for my dad when I see him later and just like that it didn't matter. I knew that nothing he said would make me not love him, so it all seemed so small. The point is I like being different and now I think he does too!

The End!